THE FORGOTTEN ARMY

Women's Poetry of the First World War

Edited by
Nora Jones and Liz Ward

Man pays that debt with new munificence,
Not piecemeal now, not slowly, but the old:
Not grudgingly, by the effaced thin pence,
But greatly and in gold.

Fathers of women with your honour in trust
Approve, accept, know them daughters of men,
Now that your sons are dust.

Alice Meynell

Highgate Publications (Beverley) Ltd., 1991

DEDICATION

To our mothers, daughters and sisters; Violet, Mary, Kate, Anna, Becky, Katharine, Linda and Jane, and remembering Sarah.

With love to Pete, David and Keith.

British Library Cataloguing in Publication Data

The forgotten army: women's poetry of the First World War.
I. Jones, Nora, II. Ward, Liz.
821.91209358

ISBN 0948929502

Published by Highgate Publications (Beverley) Ltd.
24 Wylies Road, Beverley, HU17 7AP
Telephone (0482) 866826

Printed and Typeset in 10 on 11 pt Plantin by
B.A. Press, Unit 7A, Tokenspire Park, Hull Road, Woodmansey, Beverley, HU17 0TB
Telephone (0482) 882232

CONTENTS

PREFACE

The idea that became this collection of photographs and poems was born out of curiosity. We were both working on different aspects of literature and the First World War, but, whichever way our studies led us, we finished up asking questions about what happened to the women. What were the women doing? In 1987, eager to pursue personal and research interests, we collaborated on material for a day school on Women and the First World War. A chance find in a junk shop in Gloucester provided us with an unexpected base for an exhibition. Ten bound volumes of *The War Budget*, a weekly periodical published by the *Daily Chronicle* during the war years, added a visual dimension to our view of women's involvement in the war that we were beginning to pick up from our explorations into war literature. Curiosity became fascination and we went on to search through dusty shelves in secondhand bookshops as well as libraries. From having been surprised that there were so many women war poets in Catherine Reilly's *Scars Upon My Heart*, we found that there were so many more. *Scars* was an inspiration, but the tip of an iceberg for us. Autobiographies, diaries and novels also gave an increasingly detailed picture of what war meant for all kinds of women. We hope that this anthology, linking words and images, will lead others into this rewarding area of literature and history.

November, 1991   Nora Jones
                                                      Liz Ward

INTRODUCTION

It is over seventy years since the end of the First World War, an event which is becoming history, no longer memory. The prevailing image is still that of young men sent out to the slaughter, a lost generation. Military accounts, descriptions of battles and appalling casualty figures state baldly how many men were lost. Diaries, personal accounts and fictional interpretations of experiences on active service have added individual voices to official statements. The poetry of the soldier poets of the First World War has become almost as familiar as the sepia photographs of marching soldiers and the devastated landscape of the Salient and the Somme.

This is not to question the value of these images. The pictures presented are immensely moving, horrifying, courageous, humorous — the whole gamut of emotions and responses become appropriate to readings of a cross section of war literature. Yet this only tells half the story. It is surprising that the literature and history of that era has been related with so little reference to women's perceptions of the war years, and that only a relatively small amount of their writing has been given the attention it deserves.

Most anthologies of war poetry include no, or few, poems by women, yet they, too, wrote of their war: one of equal grief and uncertainty, empathy with the men, pride and protest, and a shared knowledge of loss and futility. Although some of their work appeared in journals and small volumes published during the war, very few have remained in print. There is, therefore, no tradition of women's war poetry and it disappeared soon after the war. It was not until 1981 when Catherine Reilly's selection of women's poetry and verse of the First World War, *Scars Upon My Heart*, was published by Virago, that any real attention was given to it. What was clear from this volume, was that most of it was written out of a need to express the events, or their perceptions of them, as they happened. It was not 'emotion recollected in tranquillity' but more an immediate expression of exceptional circumstance. For Wilfred Owen, the poetry was 'in the pity'. There is pity here in plenty, but there is creative skill and sensibility, courage, humour and sometimes bitter irony too, amply demonstrating that the poetry is also in the poetry.

The poetry sheds a little light on the lives of this often forgotten army of women, because, whether or not they were moved by patriotism, public opinion, pressure from families or the spirit of adventure, many women were caught up in the machinery of war. For those at home, 'doing one's bit' meant rolling bandages, working on the land or in a munitions factory or simply looking after the family. For those at the Front, it meant sharing appalling conditions and dealing with the consequences of war's destruction. For most, it was a time of grief and the stress of waiting for news, casualty figures or letters. For all, a way of life was changed.

Collectively, women's own words and images help to contradict popular assumptions that their roles were to knit socks, keep the home fires burning and browbeat men into the Forces. They also dissipate notions of women's ignorance of the realities of war and show how intimately they shared the anguish of those years.

The poems, like the photographs, stand as a memorial to their experience.

THESE WERE
THE SPLENDID DAYS

THESE were the Splendid Days,
   And they are fled,
Now go we lonely ways,
Our Loves are dead:
Only the vision stays
And the word said.

Now never Splendid Days
The years will bring,
Now go we lonely ways
Remembering:
Still with the Lover stays
The given ring.

May Wedderburn Cannan

THE RECRUIT

HIS mother bids him go without a tear;
   His sweetheart walks beside him proudly gay,
"No coward have I loved," her clear eyes say—
The band blares out and all the townsfolk cheer.

Yet in his heart he thinks: "I am afraid!
I am afraid of Fear — how can I tell
If in the ordeal 'twill go ill or well?
How can man tell how bravely man is made?"

Steady he waits, obeying brisk command,
Head up, chin firm, and every muscle steeled,—
Thinking: "I shot a rabbit in a field
And sickened at its blood upon my hand."

The sky is blue and little winds blow free,
He catches up his comrades' marching-song;
Their bayonets glitter as they sweep along—
("How ghastly a *red* bayonet must be!").

How the folk stare! His comrade on the right
Whispers a joke — is gay and debonair,
Sure of himself and quite at odds with care;—
But does he, too, turn restlessly at night?

From each familiar scene his inner eye
Turns to far fields by Titans rent and torn;
For in that struggle must his soul be born,
To look upon itself and live — or die!

Isabel Ecclestone Mackay

THE CALL TO ARMS IN OUR STREET

THERE'S a woman sobs her heart out,
   With her head against the door,
For the man that's called to leave her,
   —God have pity on the poor!
      But it's beat, drums, beat,
      While the lads march down the street,
      And it's blow, trumpets, blow,
      Keep your tears until they go.

There's a crowd of little children
   Who march along and shout,
For it's fine to play at soldiers
   Now their fathers are called out.
      So it's beat, drums, beat;
      But who'll find them food to eat?
      And it's blow, trumpets, blow,
      Ah! the children little know.

There's a mother who stands watching
   For the last look of her son,
A worn poor widow woman,
   And he her only one.
      But it's beat, drums, beat,
      Though God knows when we shall meet;
      And it's blow, trumpets, blow:
      We must smile and cheer them so.

There's a young girl who stands laughing,
   For she thinks a war is grand,
And it's fine to see the lads pass,
   And it's fine to hear the band.
      So it's beat, drums, beat,
      To the fall of many feet;
      And it's blow, trumpets, blow,
      God go with you where you go!

Winifred M. Letts

3

THE DAY'S WORK

Dedicatory for an Office Magazine

WE bring you merchandise
  From near and far,
Who have grown very wise
And old in War.

We know our hearts' desires,
How strong they be:
We would build our camp-fires
From sea to sea.

We know our hands, their power,
These too we give:
And our lives' little hour
Whereby we live.

We bring small merchandise
When all is said:
We pray our day's work buys
Our daily bread.

May Wedderburn Cannan

GREY KNITTING

SOMETHING sings gently through the din of the battle,
    Something spreads very softly rim on rim,
And every soldier hears, at times, a murmur
Tender, incessant, — dim.

A tiny click of little wooden needles,
Elfin amid the gianthood of war;
Whispers of women, tireless and patient,
Who weave the web afar.

Whispers of women — tireless and patient,
"This is our heart's love," it would seem to say,
"Wrought with the ancient tools of our vocation,
Weave we the web of love from day to day."

And so each soldier, laughing, fighting, — dying
Under the alien skies, in his great hour,
May listen, in death's prescience all-enfolding,
And hear a fairy sound bloom like a flower—

I like to think that soldiers, gaily dying
For the white Christ on fields with shame sown deep,
May hear the tender song of women's needles,
As they fall fast asleep.

Katherine Hale

*Someone has evolved the ingenious idea of knitting
a waistcoat in black and white squares, so that it
can be used at the front for playing chess or draughts.
Our photograph shows it "in action".*

*Battersea school children have knitted large quantities of socks for our soldiers at the front. They gave
a performance at the Grand Theatre, Clapham, to raise further funds. Photograph shows them
rehearsing their part, "Knitting Socks for Soldiers".*

NOSTRA CULPA

WE knew, this thing at least we knew, — the worth
    Of life: this was our secret learned at birth.
We knew that Force the world has deified,
How weak it is. We spoke not, so men died.
Upon a world down-trampled, blood-defiled,
Fearing that men should praise us less, we smiled.

We knew the sword accursed, yet with the strong
Proclaimed the sword triumphant. Yea, this wrong
Unto our children, unto those unborn
We did, blaspheming God. We feared the scorn
Of men; men worshipped pride; so were they led,
We followed. Dare we now lament our dead?

Shadows and echoes, harlots! We betrayed
Our sons; because men laughed we were afraid.
That silent wisdom which was ours we kept
Deep-buried; thousands perished; still we slept.
Children were slaughtered, women raped, the weak
Down-trodden. Very quiet was our sleep.

Ours was the vision, but the vision lay
Too far, too strange; we chose an easier way.
The light, the unknown light, dazzled our eyes. —
Oh! sisters in our choice were we not wise?
When all men hated, could we pity or plead
For love with those who taught the Devil's creed?

Reap we with pride the harvest! it was sown
By our own toil. Rejoice! it is our own.
This is the flesh we might have saved — our hands,
Our hands prepared these blood-drenched, dreadful lands.
What shall we plead? That we were deaf and blind?
We mothers and we murderers of mankind.

Margaret Sackville

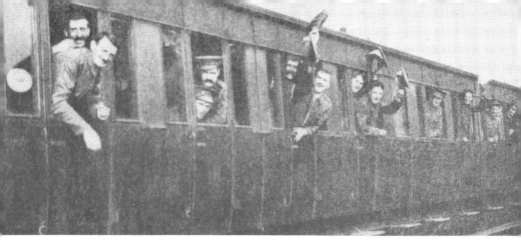

A SOLDIER'S FACE IN A STARTING TRAIN

CLAMOUR and shout,
　　And the long, packed train quite slowly moving out.
Some cried farewell,
Some with their tears told all they had to tell.
A muff, a swinging cap, a body's grace,
A waving hand,
And, like some weeping heart, the gaiety of the band;
Then, through the crowd, the loneliness of your face,
Glimpsed for a moment only: lost and gone
As the train went moving on.

Almost it seemed
You looked out from the train as one who dreamed
And watched some phantom show's queer pageant flit,
And were lonely, outside, watching it.

Just what you left — maybe had not to leave —
Of hearts to hope and grieve,
Just what you lost, won, dreaded, hoped to win,
These made your secret which your face locked in;
Your only testament
To me — you heard the call, and went.

With the turbulence and din
Of battle hammering near you, clipping you in;
A man's life as lightly going
As a wind's blowing;
Your life as like to be cut off as not
In the sore stress;
For all, be it much or little, that you gave,
God give you comfort in your inmost thought,
Vision and knowledge of what you fight to save,
And in that vision break your loneliness.

Agnes Grozier Herbertson

TRAINS IN FRANCE

ALL through the night among the unseen hills
    The trains,
The fire-eyed trains,
Call to each other their wild seeking cry,
And I,
Who thought I had forgotten all the War,
Remember now a night in Camiers,
When, through the darkness, as I wakeful lay,
I heard the trains,
The savage, shrieking trains,
Call to each other their fierce hunting-cry,
Ruthless, inevitable, as the beasts
After their prey.
Made for this end by their creators, they,
Whose business was to capture and devour
Flesh of our flesh, bone of our very bone.
Hour after hour,
Angry and impotent I lay alone
Hearing them hunt you down, my dear, and you,
Hearing them carry you away to die,
Trying to warn you of the beasts, the beasts!
Then, no, thought I;
So foul a dream as this cannot be true,
And calmed myself, hearing their cry no more.
Till, from the silence, broke a trembling roar,
And I heard, far away,
The growling thunder of their joyless feasts —
The beasts had got you then, the beasts, the beasts —
And knew
The nightmare true.

Winifred Holtby

9

LUNCH HOUR

WITHDRAWN for a little space from the confusion
    Of pulled potatoes littered on broken earth,
We lay in the shadowed ditch, a peaceful circle
      Of food, drink, smoke, and mirth.

The smell of the ditch was hot and sweet, and heavy
    With poppy flowers, and tangled with nettle-weed.
In the grass a cricket chirped his eternal question,
      Like a thin tune on a reed.

Blue tobacco-smoke drifted and curled about us;
    Its eddying wove for us a mystic screen.
The field and its littered trenches dropped, and shimmered
      In the clear gulf between

Real and dream; the gulf where shadowless silence
    Dwells and beauty is strange, and thin, and far,
And the world is quiet and flat, as pictures woven
      On old tapestries are.

So we lay and laughed in the breathless noon-tide.
    Your laughter, and your faces, burnt with the sun,
Were as far and as near as heaven, and as mystic. . . .
      And the lunch hour was done.

Stiffly we stooped again in the sun-baked trenches,
    And flung the lifted potatoes into pails.
And the earth stood out once more in relief and shadow,
      Wholesome, like fairy-tales.

Rose Macaulay

THE SCARLET HARVEST

SCARLET waves the harvest, waiting for the
reaping,
Nourished with the blood of dead heroes who
lie sleeping,
Hush your laughter, ye who pass; whisper softly
and tread slowly;
God's acre, field and meadow, all around the
ground is holy.

Fighting in the front rank, dying where they fell,
In the din and roar of battle, in the carnage
that was Hell;
Writhing in their anguish with gaping wounds
and gory,
Resting now in peace and everlasting glory.

Gentlemen and rankers, soldiers one and all
the same,
When their Captain sounds the roll-call each
will answer to his name.
Foolish people, cease your weeping — nay, be
proud your dead are sleeping —
Gather in the scarlet harvest, ye are honoured
in the reaping.

Valerie L. Esson

A FATHER OF WOMEN

AD SOROREM E. B.

'Thy father was transfused into thy blood.'
DRYDEN: *Ode to Mrs. Anne Killigrew*

OUR father works in us,
The daughters of his manhood. Not undone
Is he, not wasted, though transmuted thus,
        And though he left no son.

Therefore on him I cry
To arm me: 'For my delicate mind a casque,
A breastplate for my heart, courage to die,
        Of thee, captain, I ask.

'Nor strengthen only; press
A finger on this violent blood and pale,
Over this rash will let they tenderness
        A while pause, and prevail.

'And shepherd-father, thou
Whose staff folded my thoughts before my bir
Control them now I am of earth, and now
        Thou art no more of earth.

'O liberal, constant, dear,
Crush in my nature the ungenerous art
Of the inferior; set me high, and here,
        Here garner up thy heart!'

Like to him now are they,
The million living fathers of the War—
Mourning the crippled world, the bitter day—
        Whose striplings are no more.

The crippled world! Come then,
Fathers of women with your honour in trust,
Approve, accept, know them daughters of me:
        Now that your sons are dust.

Alice Meynell

"MISSING"

Ben Rowlands, Llanfair Forge, September 1914

BY Llanfair Church the smithy stands,
 And there, for ages past,
Father and son, with strength and skill,
 Farm-horses' shoes have cast.

And in the chapel up the hill
 Have preached and sung and prayed.
But now at Minfford, by His will,
 God's soldiers' shells are made.

So Ben has gone from forge and home,
 To take his strenuous share
In shaping shell and bolt and bomb,
 Till righteous Peace shines fair.

Helen E. Phillp

DEDICATION *(To a Field Ambulance in Flanders)*

I do not call you comrades,
   You,
Who did what I only dreamed.
Though you have taken my dream,
And dressed yourselves in its beauty and its glory,
Your faces are turned aside as you pass by.
I am nothing to you,
For I have done no more than dream.

Your faces are like the face of her whom you follow,
Danger,
The Beloved who looks backward as she runs, calling
   to her lovers,
The Huntress who flies before her quarry, trailing her
   lure.
She called to me from her battle-places,
She flung before me the curved lightning of her shells
   for a lure;
And when I came within sight of her,
She turned aside,
And hid her face from me.

But you she loved;
You she touched with her hand;
For you the white flames of her feet stayed in their
   running;
She kept you with her in her fields of Flanders,
Where you go,
Gathering your wounded from among her dead.
Grey night falls on your going and black night on your
   returning.
You go
Under the thunder of the guns, the shrapnel's rain and
   the curved lightning of the shells,
And where the high towers are broken,
And houses crack like the staves of a thin crate filled
   with fire;
Into the mixing smoke and dust of roof and walls torn
   asunder
You go;
And only my dream follows you.

That is why I do not speak of you,
Calling you by your names.
Your names are strung with the names of ruined and
   immortal cities,
Termonde and Antwerp, Dixmude and Ypres and
   Furnes,
Like jewels on one chain—

Thus,
In the high places of Heaven,
They shall tell all your names.   *May Sinclair*

HOSPITAL SANCTUARY

WHEN you have lost your all in a world's upheaval,
    Suffered and prayed, and found your prayers were vain,
When love is dead, and hope has no renewal —
These need you still; come back to them again.

When the sad days bring you the loss of all ambition,
And pride is gone that gave you strength to bear,
When dreams are shattered, and broken is all decision —
Turn you to these, dependent on your care.

They too have fathomed the depths of human anguish,
Seen all that counted flung like chaff away;
The dim abodes of pain wherein they languish
Offer that peace for which at last you pray.

Vera Brittain

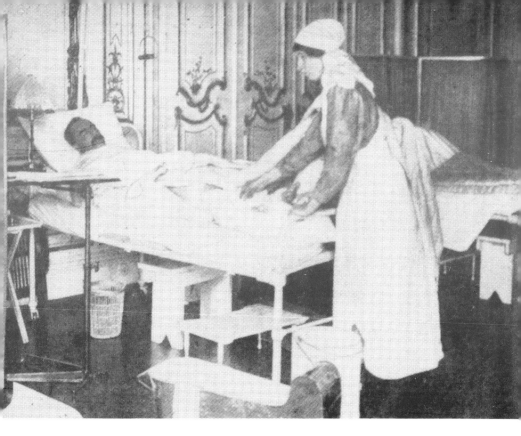

BESIDE THE BED

SOMEONE has shut the shining eyes, straightened and folded
   The wandering hands quietly covering the unquiet breast:
So, smoothed and silenced you lie, like a child not again to be questioned or scolded;
   But, for you, not one of us believes that this is rest.

Not so to close the windows down can cloud and deaden
   The blue beyond: or to screen the wavering flame subdue its breath:
Why, if I lay my cheek to your cheek, your grey lips, like dawn, would quiver and
     redden,
   Breaking into the old, odd smile at this fraud of death.

Because all night you have not turned to us or spoken
   It is time for you to wake; your dreams were never very deep:
I, for one, have seen the thin, bright, twisted threads of them dimmed suddenly and
     broken,
   This is only a most piteous pretence of sleep!

Charlotte Mew

THE MOTHER

H ER boys are not shut out. They come
    Homing like pigeons to her door,
Sure of her tender welcome home,
    As many a time before.

Their bed is made so smooth and sweet,
    The fire is lit — the table spread;
She has poured water for their feet,
    That they be comforted.

As with a fluttering of wings
    They are come home, come home to stay;
With all the bitter dreadful things
    Forgot, clean washed away.

They are so glad to stay, so glad
    They nestle to her gown's soft flow,
As in the loving times they had,
    Long ago, long ago.

Oh, not like lonely ghosts in mist
    Her boys come from the night and rain,
But to be clasped, but to be kissed,
    And not go out again.

Katherine Tynan

THE MOTHER

Written after reading Rupert Brooke's sonnet, 'The Soldier':

> If I should die, think only this of me:
> That there's some corner of a foreign field
> That is for ever England.

I F you should die, think only this of me
  In that still quietness where is space for thought,
Where parting, loss and bloodshed shall not be,
And men may rest themselves and dream of nought:
That in some place a mystic mile away
One whom you loved has drained the bitter cup
Till there is nought to drink; has faced the day
Once more, and now, has raised the standard up.

And think, my son, with eyes grown clear and dry
She lives as though for ever in your sight,
Loving the things *you* loved, with heart aglow
For country, honour, truth, traditions high,
— Proud that you paid their price. (And if some night
Her heart should break — well, lad, you will not know.)

May Herschel-Clarke

NINE BROTHERS SERVING KING AND COUNTRY

Mrs. Lahee, who lives at Winchmore Hill, has no fewer than nine sons who are now doing their duty "for King and Country". She has received a letter from Sir Frederick Ponsonby expressing the King's appreciation of the family's splendid spirit of patriotism. Our picture shows Mrs. Lahee with eight of her sons and her three daughters. The names of the brothers serving and their corps are: Henry Lahee, Union Defence Force, South Africa; Herbert Lahee, 2nd King Edward's Horse; Frank Lahee, now in France with the Queen Victoria Rifles; Terence Lahee, also in France with the same regiment; Sidney Lahee, in Malta with the 3rd Royal Fusiliers (City of London Regiment); Roy Lahee, Royal Canadian Rifles, Bermuda; Arthur Lahee, Union Defence Force, South Africa; Edward Lahee, 2nd King Edward's Horse; and Percy Lahee, Royal Field Artillery. All were taught their drill in the Boys' Brigade.

From THE TRIBUTE

WE will choose for each lad of the city,
 a flower or a spray of grass—

For the lads who drew apart,
the scholar and poet we place
wind-flower or lily or wreath
of ivy and crocus shaft,
and the lads who went to slay
with passion and thirst,
we give roses and flowers of bay.

That the lads in that city apart
may know of our love and keep
remembrance and speak of us—
may lift their hands that the gods
revisit earth.

That the lads of the cities
may yet remember us,
we spread shaft of privet and sweet
lily from meadow and forest,
and the wild white lily,
and the wood-lily,
and the red shaft from the mountain-side.

H.D.

WHAT BURSTING SHELLS LOOK LIKE
This remarkable photograph, which was taken recently in Flanders, shows three German shells bursting simultaneously over a village. The dense cloud of smoke on the left was caused by a "Jack Johnson".

HIGH SUMMER

PINKS and syringa in the garden closes,
   And the sweet privet hedge and golden roses,
The pines hot in the sun, the drone of the bee,
They die in Flanders to keep these for me.

The long sunny days and the still weather,
The cuckoo and blackbird shouting together,
The lambs calling their mothers out on the lea,
They die in Flanders to keep these for me.

All doors and windows open: the South wind blowing
Warm through the clean sweet rooms on tiptoe going,
Where many sanctities, dear and delightsome, be,
They die in Flanders to keep these for me.

Daisies leaping in foam on the green grasses,
The dappled sky and the stream that sings as it passes;
These are bought with a price, a bitter fee,
They die in Flanders to keep these for me.

                   Katherine Tynan

HOMES

THE lamplight's shaded rose
   On couch and chair and wall,
The drowsy book let fall,
The children's heads, bent close
In some deep argument,
The kitten, sleepy-curled,
Sure of our good intent,
The hearth-fire's crackling glow:
His step that crisps the snow,
His laughing kiss, wind-cold. . .

Only the very old
Gifts that the night-star brings,
Dear homely evening-things,
Dear things of all the world,
And yet my throat locks tight. . . . .

Somewhere far off I know
Are ashes on red snow
That were a home last night.

        Margaret Widdemer

A PRIVATE

WHAT did his mother give, who bore
     Him in her unripe womb
An ugly child, to whom
No secret lurked behind the brothel door?

Hard are Life's gifts to understand!
He found her, an old whore
Drunken upon the floor
Rolling her hair in the foul spattered sand.

She gave him curses twice or thrice
While "son" boomed in her brain,
Then fell to trade again
And shouted words about her body's price.

What did life show but gaslit hell,
Walked by the battered dead
Smouldering black and red
Where the fire glowed under their reek and smell?

With the beloved and fortunate
He shares his earthy bed.
The maggots breed, where bred
His slow thoughts, and their thoughts for ever animate.

I heard the funeral trumpet ring
Above the mourning throng
To match that song
Of universal grief, what could thought bring?

Lucy Hawkins

24

TO AN OFFICER IN REGENT STREET

L IKE some lean ghost who for a little space
   Looks on the world again, and the clear skies,
Or mariner that from the sea doth rise
In vain, to find another in his place,
You walk with shades of death on your brown face
And look upon the street with dead men's eyes.

Fresh women throng beside you in the street
And painted women; but they seek in vain
To catch those haunted eyes, or turn again
From their slow course toward waiting death your feet.
You must pass lonely, on whose brow there meet
Abel's sharp anguish, and the curse of Cain.

Lucy Hawkins

AT PARTING

IT was sad weather when you went away,
   Wind, and the rain was raining every day.
And all night long I heard in lonesome sleep
The water running under the bows of the ship,
All the dark night and till the dawning grey.

At Salonika it is golden weather.
Go light of heart, O child, light as a feather,
   Valiant and full of laughter, free as air.
   God is at Salonika — here and there
God and my heart are keeping watch together.

But O when you come back, though skies should weep,
The water running under the bows of the ship
   Shall in my dreams make music exquisite
   And my all happy sleep be drenched with it,
And you coming home, home through the hours of
      sleep.

Katharine Tynan

26

SMILE, DEATH

S MILE, Death, see I smile as I come to you
    Straight from the road and the moor that I leave behind,
Nothing on earth to me was like this wind-blown space,
Nothing was like the road, but at the end there was a vision or a face
    And the eyes were not always kind.

    Smile, Death, as you fasten the blades to my feet for me,
On, on let us skate past the sleeping willows dusted with snow;
Fast, fast down the frozen stream, with the moor and the road and the vision behind,
    (Show me your face, why the eyes are kind!)
And we will not speak of life or believe in it or remember it as we go.

Charlotte Mew

HERE LIES A PRISONER

L EAVE him: he's quiet enough: and what matter
    Out of his body or in, you can scatter
The frozen breath of his silenced soul, of his outraged soul to the winds that rave
Quieter now than he used to be, but listening still to the magpie chatter
    Over his grave.

Charlotte Mew

THE GATE

THERE is no smell of dust
　　On the road that leads to the farm,
But the bitter breath of the woody must.
(The red round moon very soon will thrust
　　Over the long hill's arm.)

I shall come, at the wood's end,
To the cart-track over the hill;
And the open hill is a kindly friend.
(Over my head the birch-trees bend,
　　Silver, and grave, and still.)

At the wood-road's end is a gate;
And (though there is no one there)
They who have passed through it dark and late
Say it creaks and groans, as under a weight
　　That is heavy and ill to bear.

The path twists so suddenly
That you cannot see far ahead.
But when you have come to the old thorn tree
(I am close to it now) then you may see
　　The gate, with its broken tread. . . .

With a hand pressed over each eye
Some men have pushed through blind . . .
But then should I surely run mad and die
If I was touched, as I stumbled by,
　　By a hand reached out behind. . . .

　　★　　★　　★　　★　　★

They found him running in the hill country,
Full many a long hour's journey from that place.
No tale he told, but gibbered crazily,
And ran and ran, as he would win a race.

And the moon had dried his tears upon his face.

Rose Macaulay

THE ARMISTICE
In an Office, in Paris

THE news came through over the telephone:
    All the terms had been signed: The War was
        won:
And all the fighting and the agony,
And all the labour of the years were done.
One girl clicked sudden at her typewriter
And whispered, 'Jerry's safe', and sat and stared:
One said, 'It's over, over, it's the end:
The War is over: ended': and a third,
'I can't remember life without the war'.
And one came in and said, 'Look here, they say
We can all go at five to celebrate,
As long as two stay on, just for to-day'.

It was quite quiet in the big empty room
Among the typewriters and little piles
Of index cards: one said, 'We'd better just
Finish the day's reports and do the files'.
And said, 'It's awf'lly like *Recessional*,
Now when the tumult has all died away'.
The other said, 'Thank God we saw it through;
I wonder what they'll do at home to-day'.
And said, 'You know it will be quiet to-night
Up at the Front: first time in all these years,
And no one will be killed there any more',
And stopped to hide her tears.
She said, 'I've told you; he was killed in June'.
The other said, 'My dear, I know; I know . . .
It's over for me too . . . My Man was killed,
Wounded . . . and died . . . at Ypres . . . three
        years ago . . .
And he's my Man, and I want him', she said,
And knew that peace could not give back her
        Dead.

*Second-Lieutenant Harris and Miss E.
Lagon Sibbald, who have just been
married at Peper Harow, Godalming.
Lieutenant Harris gained a commission
for bravery on the field. He came home,
was married by special licence, and
returned to the battlefield the next day.*

*TELEPHONE OPERATORS'
ROMANCE
Sergeant F. Mallows, R.E., and his
bride were both popular members of the
staff of the London Telephone Trunk
Exchange. The gallant sergeant has
been in France since last November. He
obtained leave on Friday morning
recently, was married on Monday, and
was back in France on the Friday
morning following.*

WOMEN DEMOBILIZED

July 1919

NOW must we go again back to the world
    Full of grey ghosts and voices of men dying,
And in the rain the sounding of Last Posts,
And Lovers' crying—
Back to the old, back to the empty world.

Now are put by the bugles and the drums,
And the worn spurs, and the great swords they carried,
Now are we made most lonely, proudly, theirs,
The men we married:
Under the dome the long roll of the drums.

Now are the Fallen happy and sleep sound,
Now, in the end, to us is come the paying,
These who return will find the love they spend,
But we are praying
Love of our Lovers fallen who sleep sound.

Now in our hearts abides always our war,
Time brings, to us, no day for our forgetting,
Never for us is folded War away,
Dawn or sun setting,
Now in our hearts abides always our war.

May Wedderburn Cannan

ACKNOWLEDGEMENTS

We would like to thank the following for permission to reprint some of the poems in this anthology:—

Vera Brittain, Hospital Sanctuary, from *Verses of a VAD* and Winifred Holtby, Trains in France from *The Frozen Earth* reprinted by permission of Mr. Paul Berry, literary executor of both authors.

H.D., We will choose for each lad of the city......from *The Tribute, Collected Poems* reprinted by permission of Carcanet Press Ltd.

Rose Macauley, Lunch Hour and The Gate from *Three Days* reprinted by permission of Peters, Frazer & Dunlop.

May Sinclair, Dedication, from *A Journal of Impressions in Belgium* reprinted by permission of the literary executors of May Sinclair's estate.

May Wedderburn Cannan, The Armistice, The Day's Work, These were the Splendid Days and Women Demobilized, from *In War Time* and *These were the Splendid Days* reprinted by permission of Mr. James Slater.

We have made every effort to contact publishers, literary executors and copyright holders of all the material used and offer our apologies to any whom we have been unable to locate.

We would also like to thank the Department of Adult and Continuing Education and the Library of Hull University and the Imperial War Museum for their invaluable help and resources in compiling this anthology.

BIBLIOGRAPHY

BRITTAIN Vera (1896-1970) Hospital Sanctuary, *Verses of a VAD*, McDonald, 1918.

DOOLITTLE Hilda (H.D.) (1886-1961) We will choose for each lad of the city, from *The Tribute*, *H.D. Collected Poems* Carcanet, 1954.

ECCLESTON Mackay Isabel (1875-1928) The Recruit, *A Treasury of War Poetry*, Clarke G. H. (Ed.), Hodder & Stoughton, 1917.

ESSON Valerie, The Scarlet Harvest, *The Lyceum Book of War Verse*, Erskine McDonald Ltd., 1918.

GROZIER-HERBERTSON Agnes, A Soldier's Face in a Starting Train, from 'The Windsor Magazine', Vol XLIII, Ward & Lock, 1916.

HALE, Katherine (1878-1956) Grey Knitting, *A Treasury of War Poetry*, 1917.

HAWKINS Lucy, A private
     To an Officer in Regent Street
At a Venture, Blackwell, 1917.

HERSCHEL-CLARKE May, The Mother, *Poetry of the Great War*, Dominic Hibberd, John Onions (Eds.) Macmillan, 1986.

HOLTBY Winifred (1898-1935) Trains in France, *The Frozen Earth*, Collins, 1935.

LETS Winifred M. (1882-1971) The Call to Arms in our Street, *A Treasury of War Poetry*, 1917.

MACAULAY Rose (1889-1958) Lunch Hour
        The Gate
Three Days, Constable & Co, 1919.

MEW Charlotte (1869-1928) Beside the Bed
        Here Lies a Prisoner
        Smile, Death
Collected Poems, Gerald Duckworth & Co., 1953.

MEYNELL Alice (1847-1922) A Father of Women
        In Time of War
Selected Poems of Alice Meynell, Nonesuch Press, 1965.

PHILLP Helen, Missing, *The Lyceum Book of War Verse*, 1918.

SACKVILLE Margaret (1881-1963) Nostra Culpa, *Collected Poems*, Martin Secker, 1939.

SINCLAIR May (1865-1946) Dedication (To a Field Ambulance in Flanders), *Journal of Impressions in Belgium*, Hutchinson, 1915.

TYNAN Katharine (1861-1931) The Mother, from 'The Windsor Magazine', Vol XLV, 1916.
High Summer
At Parting,
Flower of Youth, Sidgwick & Jackson, 1915.

WEDDERBURN CANNAN May (1863-1973) The Day's Work, *In War Time*, Blackwell, 1917.
These were the Splendid Days
The Armistice
Women Demobilized, *These were the Splendid Days*, Blackwell, 1919.

WIDDENER Margaret (1884-1976) Homes.